The Borrowed World

the

B
O
R
R
O
W
E
D

WORLD

POEMS BY
Emily Leithauser

WINNER OF THE 2015 ABLE MUSE BOOK AWARD

ABLE MUSE PRESS

Able Muse Press

www.ablemusepress.com

Printed in the United States of America

Library of Congress Control Number: 2015955768

ISBN 978-1-927409-67-1 (paperback)
ISBN 978-1-927409-68-8 (digital)

Cover image: "One View" by Alexander Pepple

Cover & book design by Alexander Pepple

Able Muse Press is an imprint of *Able Muse:* A Review of Poetry, Prose & Art—at www.ablemuse.com

Able Muse Press
467 Saratoga Avenue #602
San Jose, CA 95129

for Richie, Maggie, and Stella

Acknowledgments

I am grateful to the editors of the following journals where many of these poems originally appeared, sometimes in slightly different forms.

Able Muse: "Instinct"

Blackbird: "Shadow"

Harvard Divinity Bulletin: "Bonsai"

Iron Horse Literary Review: "And, Again, Walking with You" and "Encounter in East Coker"

Measure: "Pagoda Cinema"

New Ohio Review: "Haiku for a Divorce" and "Baltimore on Fire"

The Raintown Review: "Alzheimer's" and "Chest of Dolls"

Sewanee Theological Review: "The Leopard"

South Loop Review: "Hotel Room in Phoenix"

Southwest Review: "Ocmulgee Burial Grounds"

Unsplendid: "Boston Arboretum," "Elms," "The Drive," "Hakafot," and "The Guesthouse"

Thank you to Peter Campion and Alex Pepple, who believed in this book. Thank you to my teachers and mentors: Natasha Trethewey, Rosanna Warren, Robert Pinsky, Derek Walcott, D.A. Powell, Dan Hall, Ronald Schuchard, and Geraldine Higgins. My gratitude to Vijay Seshadri, for his confidence and generosity. To my most exacting readers and magnanimous editors: Clay Cogswell, Sara Peters, Joel Rozen, Marlo Starr, Sasha Weiss, and Ryan Wilson. To Bill Salter, who has spent many hours with the poems in this book. Thank you to my loving parents, Brad Leithauser and Mary Jo Salter, for surrounding me with poetry. To my sister, Hilary: my first friend. To my supportive Atlanta family: the Cowarts. To my fiancé, Simon, who is loyal, insightful, and fiercely compassionate: I love you.

Foreword

A REMARKABLE BOOK BY ANY MEASURE, Emily Leithauser's *The Borrowed World* is even more remarkable in light of the fact that it is the author's first book. Where many poets' first collections tend to be medleys of styles and subjects drawn from admired older poets, Leithauser's is remarkably unified in content and written in a carefully cultivated style. Where many first books are showy in manner and extravagant of metaphor, hers is characterized throughout by quiet authority and precise description. Apt as it is in thematic terms, her book's title has an unintended ironic dimension, in that the world she creates in *The Borrowed World* is entirely her own.

Every poem provides evidence of Leithauser's extraordinary technical skill, from the subtle but wrenching indirectness of "Haiku for a Divorce" to the smooth pentameters and seemingly effortless rhymes of "Trip to Alcatraz" to the idiosyncratically structured, masterfully executed sonnet "The Leopard." At times her technical fluency is all the more extraordinary for its unobtrusiveness, as in "My Mother's Riddle." The poem appears to be written in loose blank verse couplets, but closer examination shows that the end words of each pair of lines are anagrams of one another—"garden/danger," "lives/veils," and so on. Just as English-language poets have done for centuries, she has used a self-imposed formal challenge to spur herself to a memorable result.

An air of sadness permeates the volume:

the linen curtains recall your voice tonight,
recall the wordless steadiness of rain
some months ago, when I first learned how sorrow
saturates objects in a room.
("Late Night Conversation")

The title itself sets the keynote for the book's emphasis on fragility, impermanence, and loss, and the titles of its three sections—"The Guesthouse," "Privacy," and "Trespass"—underscore its recurring feelings of isolation, of not belonging, of never feeling completely at home. Powerful emotions are everywhere in these poems, but they are frequently portrayed as disruptive, better indulged in fantasy than acted upon, as in "Out of the Grotto":

Inside, a deep-set pool, silvered
with fish, where I can swim, and kick for air
and only almost drown,

or "The Undertow," in which "[t]he undertow beguiles" and

I tell you that I'll steer us through,
but something pulls and I release

your palm from mine, letting the current
comb and choke your little ribs

for half a second. Then I decide
to tug you up and lead us home.

or "Instinct," in which the speaker decides to put a wounded animal out of its misery, but is then unable to find it again, and concludes:

I place the rock back in my purse.
It's for the best—
this instinct teased,
and put to rest.

Emotional volatility threatens the stability of all relationships, whether the speaker's own love affairs or the decades-long marriage of her parents. Near the end of the book, in "Encounter in East Coker," she alludes to "the misguided search// for rapture at all costs. Or is it arrogance?/ I loved someone. Now I leave things up to chance." The most successful—and, in its way, most satisfying—relationship is one that is unconsummated:

> and we know we will never marry,
> never turn from each other;
>
> no accidents of lust or lustlessness
> will occur, and we can always live
>
> on the edge of something we cannot ruin,
> and what a tease that is, what a privilege:
>
> I am yours because I am never yours,
> and you are mine because you cannot wander—
>
> or not wander—and the body and its vagaries
> are incidents and not the story.
>
> ("And, Again, Walking with You")

Very near the end of the book, the poem "The Cut" alludes to "the lust/ unique to memory" and concludes with the assertion that "if healing is a gradual disappearance,/ then I don't want to heal from you." Here the speaker expresses a view that has been gradually emerging from the losses and instabilities that run through the collection: nurturing our memories, even—if not especially—the painful ones, is our way of holding on to what has shaped us, our way of holding on to ourselves. Earlier, in "Chest of Dolls," she looks through the wooden chest containing the dolls that she and her older sister had played with, recalling how "[f]or years their little ecstasies/ were more authentic than our own" and asking herself "when did their lips/ stop moving, the staples in their joints/ appear?" Remembering when her sister had outgrown the dolls, she ends the poem with lines that not only acknowledge her sister's sensitivity but also point to lessons learned about making one's way through the world:

> I understood
>
> you'd keep pretending out of love;
> for me, for them, you'd make them live
>
> as long as, humanly, you could.

I have said that *The Borrowed World* is a sad book, but reading it is far from a sad experience; it is instead a satisfying, even exhilarating one. It inspires the joy that one always feels when a skilled artist gives us a memorable portrayal of the reality we inhabit, the joy inspired by even such grim works as *King Lear* and *Waiting for Godot* because they make us say, Yes, this is how it is to be as we are and to make our way in this world. In "Haiku for Insomnia," the speaker recalls the sleepless nights of her childhood when her father would share with her a volume of Hiroshige prints. As he closed the book, he would tease her interest by saying "Tomorrow night's will amaze you." The poem concludes:

> I'm grateful
> now you taught me that suspense:
> art that waits for you.

I have read *The Borrowed World* several times, and each time I find more in it to be delighted and touched by. Emily Leithauser's art waits for you, and I am sure that you will be as pleased and moved by it as I have been.

—Michael Palma

Contents

III. Trespass

The Borrowed World

I. The Guesthouse

The Drive

Its crooked sign is a darker patch of night.
The road's so black between the fringe of pines

it could almost be your street. And I could almost
be making my way to you, the white brush

of high beams brightly fogging names I know,
catching a candle, a gesture, a flicker, a wink

in a passing window, a piece of streetlight
in the cobwebbed gap between two branches.

I don't believe, or mostly don't, but when
I pass the stubbled cornfield, frozen gray,

an hour before Christmas, the needle shaking
on the speedometer in the corner of my sight,

I consider saying a prayer, not for you,
not *Not* for you, for nothing abstract and nothing

I know, like the slight notch in the road, this
or that tree, but, unthinking, for snow.

The Guesthouse

We hold our breath in a haze of sulfur, watching
          the grass and leaves slip down our legs,
down the drain. I touch you, sensing the heat is going,

    and swallow soap behind your ear, as I kiss
          the places your beard is growing back,
then I bury my face in your neck, your collarbone. You wash

    my shoulders; I touch the dent between your ribs,
          an upturned spoon, too small to capture
the water. It's not getting colder, I want to tell you,

    as shampoo coils around your ankles, under
          your arches, between your toes like the vines
of Virginia creeper outside. And now, wrapped in a towel,

    I watch the sun set in a wine bottle,
          tipped over on the balcony,
and then the stars. Your hair is still damp; I lay you down,

    trying to meet your eyes. I should have known,
          that night, our hips knocking softly
together, my mouth on your shoulder, to meet your eyes

    for longer. We're in a wooden bed, carved for guests,
          in someone else's house, in sheets
that smell like the sawdust and wild lilies outside.

I should have made the scraps of light, shining
    from the main house into our room,
moving with our movements, into a memory.

Shadow

As the plane descends, its shadow runs
ahead, widens, spreading like a bruise,

one wing slanted toward the lit
and lettered gates below, and I remember

the hanging circles of a hawk
above the rocks, a vole or squirrel caught

in talons, beating the air. The creature
doesn't see the massive wingspan cast

its image below: a stingray coasting
slowly, closely, over uneven ground.

The prey cannot see its shadow
held inside the hawk's, or know its captor

as a deepening of water,
a darkening of rocks, or an eclipse

that wanders; cannot fear the far-off
nest—but only senses rushing air,

only knows the angled fall.

Undertow

They warned against the coming surf:
abandoned towels fringed in foam,

cabals of wind-warped parasols
tipping in the growing tide.

The undertow beguiles. We're hand
in hand, swimming through seaweed and sand.

I tell you that I'll steer us through,
but something pulls and I release

your palm from mine, letting the current
comb and choke your little ribs

for half a second. Then I decide
to tug you up and lead us home.

Instinct

Hunched, obsidian-eyed, and inches
from the curb—one paw gone, the other
 tight as a clasp—
 the animal,
 unblinking, breathes

in little rasps. Why isn't he shaking,
crawling beneath settled leaves,
 or moving toward
 the gutter, where
 it's quiet under

the sidewalk's shadow? Cars keep missing
him. You tell me a rock will do.
 A skull that small
 will crack. Nothing
 ironic in

your tone, or in the five-pound block
of cement I pretend is
 a stone. To let
 him live seems coldly
 primitive.

But when I'm ready I can't find him;
I jump at stirring leaves; I pass
      a shadow, no,
      a flat, gray thing
      which wind rustles

and seems to animate again.
I place the rock back in my purse.
      It's for the best—
      this instinct teased,
      and put to rest.

Reservoir

Returning to a hot apartment filled
    with ladybugs and dust,

    I remember swimming toward
the line of distant, blue-green mist

across the reservoir, and how the cold
    reddened every inch

    of raised pale skin I lowered
into the water. You, dozing on the beach

on our shared towel. The water seemed to unfold
    itself, revealing more

    water. Solitude.
I wanted to lose the voices on the shore,

to swim away. Back here, my nights are filled
    with time to wonder why

    our final words were cold,
with hours to watch the hours amplify.

Out of the Grotto

I thought I heard a bear lumbering
toward me, down the wooded slope.
You had gone ahead and left me there,
behind a trap of vines.
The bear clicked against the stones,
breathing in the bushes.
The lagoon roiled with fish.
On tiptoe, I left the water and found the trail.
I opened my mouth to call your name,
but stopped when I saw your raised palm.
Had you heard my voice and thought
I'd jostle it out of camouflage?
I realized my fear was tame.
Your hand was there to hold.
The water is cold, but watched by someone
I love, who knows and guards this cove.
Inside, a deep-set pool, silvered
with fish, where I can swim, and kick for air
and only almost drown.

Fallen Elm

The storm came through. It didn't wake me.
It bent the tree that bent the fence in two.

Now its braided roots look like a spring
propelling something forward—a frozen

torquing motion—or a guitar string pulled
inward, waiting to become a note.

Its torso twists over the chain-link fence,
its leaves mingling with the tall grass

when all they've known is sky. And now
I can touch what we will never have

the balance to climb to. Stumbling on the buckled
sidewalk, the coughed-up dirt, I wonder

at the roots still half-submerged and stretching,
a little dazzled that something old,

something strong, can bend. Was it
too much? Did I learn to curve around you

too well? What you left is smooth and cold,
whittled into a holding shape,

an upturned hollow, barely deep enough
for the rain to fill.

Boston Arboretum

A baby hawk—
the nib of its beak pink—
picks at rabbit gut.
      Ribboned innards,

      dropped in flight,
lie further down the path;
I wipe my shoes on grass.
      The only sounds:

      the pluck on strings
of tripe, the ragged catch
of air in someone's throat.
      (Watch how the bird

      screens its prey
with a wing, and leaves the fur
alone, dear, and abstains
      from opening

      the cooling back.)
Even now your throat's
a thrill; your body's still
      unknown to me.

The Riddle

The rain, which we didn't hear
begin, ruined the book
propping the window open,
fell on the loosely tied
trash bags out front, and delayed
your leaving. We stayed inside

for half an hour; I loaned
you a sweater (the blue one
with holes). A little wine,
a crust of bread, and you
telling me a riddle
I still, sometimes, walk through,

on rainy nights when I
imagine we'd had a child
who waits to hear the answer,
who finds a good excuse
not to play close to me
until I'm of some use.

And, Again, Walking with You

for Richie Hofmann

Burst blossoms, shrimp-pink and swollen,
rain-heavy, green haze:

and we walk, already remembering
future walks, months from now,

when the days will narrow into flame-thin slivers
and leaves will spin, mandarin and gold,

to the ground and its pulped heaps.
So we take cover, like two betrothed

under the chuppah of a cherry orchard,
latticed with stitches of rain,

and we know we will never marry,
never turn from each other;

no accidents of lust or lustlessness
will occur, and we can always live

on the edge of something we cannot ruin,
and what a tease that is, what a privilege:

I am yours because I am never yours,
and you are mine because you cannot wander—

or not wander—and the body and its vagaries
are incidents and not the story.

Elms

for C.

Driving through the dead stump,
    the newer trunk
    (knotted, supple,
patterned by its own reflected leaves)
twists, like Michelangelo's
    half-done slaves

who seem to shake the stone
    they came from. And yet
    every year
the crown of the elm is farther from the ground,
and in the canopy the tree forgets
    that it is bound,

so that two summers from today
    (when you and I
    have left this park),
its upper reaches may entirely lose
the soundless crackle of the stump
    it split to rise.

II. Privacy

Haiku for a Divorce

to my father

1.

Three brothers in black,
the fourth, my father, eclipsed
by a stray gesture—

my grandpa, ruddy
with liquor, telling them, Keep
still for the picture.

After, you can go play
on the beach, dip your toes in,
watch your wading feet

disappear under,
as the dark room floats you up
from the black water.

2.

Back to back, sunglassed,
posed like aspiring rock stars,
we didn't know yet

what you'd do, or why
the dark-haired woman you chose
would not be enough.

3.

Sleeping in the crook
of your arm I can sense my
mother in your shirt.

4.

Luring me away
from the parked car with rumors
of veiled waterfalls

we shouldn't forget
to see, you leave me behind,
in volcano flowers.

5.

Winter in Iceland:
he walks her through morning to
a school she can't see.

6.

June, Deep South: crickets
loud as nutcrackers. Inside,
he tells her stories.

7.

I woke up to plots
you invented; fell asleep
to the crackling scenes

you had memorized,
the hushed glow of black-and-white
movies: jazz music,

the tinny '30s
laughter of Fred and Ginger,
your loud, hidden life.

Even if I knew
you watched the same old movies
most nights—their brittle,

naïve scripted smiles
projected on you, asleep,
your profile lit blue—

I never knew how
one could learn such innocence.
You tried to rewind.

8.

The novel you wrote
is signed in the used bookstore
I've found to avoid

the early spring heat,
in the city I told you
you need not visit.

9.

What is it in me,
one of your characters asks,
that seeks to destroy?

I pull your book down
and read aloud. The words blur
into a barcode.

Paragraphs lose shape,
smudge into gray. Your picture
on the jacket laughs.

Or pleads. I tilt it
on its side. I hear my voice
shaking far away—

it's like a candle,
it catches and then blows out
as soon as I move.

10.

I won't mourn the gaps
on the shelves, the keyless counter;
I won't remember

the half-eaten toast
on a bill addressed to both
of you; the cold cup

of tea; or stumbling over
your shoes in my rush to tell
you something; the wood you stacked,

hoping it would be
a cold night so you could build
a fire for us. Who

am I now that I
know this about love? It's spring.
The bicycle spokes

are covered in dust.
This winter, I hope you light
the logs of beechwood

by the hearth. Maybe
we intuited they were
too pretty to burn.

11.

You learned chemistry
again for me. Nights, you read
the textbook. You left

pencil marks. Distilled
the facts. I tried to balance
the long equations

as you did: a kind
of balance that seems destined
(now, in retrospect)

to come undone, like
strung lights hanging from
the lintel—slackened, then freed

by a rattled door.

12.

I expected you
in scrubs, but somehow it's worse:
you begin to cry,

but you're the only
well-dressed, clean-shaven patient,
with your newspaper

and shiny glasses.
You've befriended the nurses.
One presses a thumb

on your wrist. Normal.
My sister brings you a book,
a woolen blanket.

The mental health ward
is full of crayons and forms.
You have filled one out.

13.

In your handwriting:
What I most regret: doing
this to my children

14.

No running water,
one small room. Kyoto, you two,
before I was born.

And then she's pregnant—
only a couple sun-warped
photographs of her:

smiling on the street,
a proprietary hand
on her handmade dress,

a bamboo pattern,
flying geese. Or looking at
her rickety bike,

wishing she could ride.
She fed me salt and fish, tea
and roe. I waited

to be born. Sometimes
I watch over them. Holding
hands, they take a trip

to Tokyo. They stare
out from the hotel window
at Fuji. It looks

like a birthday hat,
a firecracker, maybe.
A chipped arrowhead.

Too much, now, to hold:
my young parents, such tourists
in marriage, in need

of all my watching.

My Mother's Riddle

Above their bed a painting of a garden
hangs: a fenced-in unicorn. No danger

of its galloping away. It lives
in flowers flat and stiff as bridal veils,

and can't see its shining horn. The well-kept secret
you alluded to today erects

a different fence around itself—a slip
of the tongue that separates. I watch your lips,

the hints you give, the words that hang in silence.
My thoughts gallop away. You give them license.

Mother, you speak, then stop too fast. Respond.
You leave a little girl behind who ponders

a fact her parents know and can't amend,
a secret nudged awake that can't be named.

The Lower Lake

Distance tricks us: the trees' doubles seem
to magnify their half-stripped branches, closing
      gaps of sky with reflected

      water-made, dead leaves.
From across the lake, the raveled trees
blur to something fuller. Tell me why,

though older now, you must explain away
your wrongs, or why, still listening, I nod,
      a daughter mirroring

      a tree that's disappearing.
Father, let's deny it; beautify
the growing damage: make me in your image.

Late Night Conversation

The neighbors' porch light, blurred by the rain,
the winter trees, and a splash of headlights through
the linen curtains recall your voice tonight,
recall the wordless steadiness of rain
some months ago, when I first learned how sorrow
saturates objects in a room. Holding
your familiar voice against my ear, I saw
the bricks and branches through the beaded window,
and the shifting clouds, starless and cold, until
they too became the rain, until morning
whitened and the streetlights all went out.

Tonight, you must be lying awake like me,
not wanting to talk. It doesn't matter now.
You've said the words you had to say.
I only have to turn my head to see them
hanging from the trees, to hear again
your mad refrain, asking me, or anyone,
for absolution—at my window, in the rain.

Chest of Dolls

for my sister

I open the wooden chest: an eye
knocks shut. It's musky and dark and cool

among the plastic limbs, the knots
of hair and fabric. Some are naked,

some in wrinkled skirts, their bent arms
cradling the air. Their family trees

are rolled and rubber-banded under
unsigned drawings you or I

bequeathed to the people we'd become.
For years their little ecstasies

were more authentic than our own:
I learned which smiles of yours belonged

to which of them. But when did their lips
stop moving, the staples in their joints

appear? When did we let them drop—
speaking at last face to face—

like casualties on our parents' bed?
When did I notice you were going

somewhere else? You'd grown up
without telling. I understood

you'd keep pretending out of love;
for me, for them, you'd make them live

as long as, humanly, you could.

Alzheimer's

for G.L., author of The Dinosaur Dilemma

All eloquently labeled once—objects
find ways to tease you now in vague dreams.
And you wander, docile, speechless, through the room

to your soft chair, where, for now it seems
you know you wrote the book you'd like to hear
me read aloud. Words you love. Not themes.

"The dilemma is what to do
with fossils found on someone
else's property.

In the yellow weeds, two boys
dig up the looser bones
of a blackened dinosaur."

I'm your ventriloquist, or I'm white noise,
but something budges language at your core:
my borrowed sounds your rediscovered toys.

Bonsai

You moved to Tokyo first, and Susan forgot
to shut your suitcase: your shirts tumbled out,
unironed themselves, lifted off the car
like kites. You sent back teacups, newspapered,
a flowered fan she opened with one shake.
When we arrived you bought us bonsai trees,
but only you knew what to do with them.
And then you lost your job, and we moved away,
leaving the trees with Japanese friends who sent
wagashi and dwindling news year after year.

Now Susan's dead, and no one will toss out
a dish sponge or a pillow. I buy you three:
two maples and one species I can't pronounce.
You'll trim the nail-sized leaves and twist the limbs
of what will soon be our inheritance.

Baltimore on Fire

I.

I wonder if the flashes are traffic lights,
or late-night ambulances reddening the gold
sycamore that half-blocks my window,

but it's a church that colors my bedroom walls.
The United Methodist at Keswick Avenue
and West Thirty-Third is burning: charred pews,

curled hymnals turning gray. Before the day
begins, the sirens start, and people come
to pantomime communal fear. Boards crack

and hiss, the fire rises to the roof,
the rafters sag, and slate shingles clatter
in the aisles. Light from the burning hollow.

II.

Baltimore in black and white on postcards,
on cheap fold-out maps, and in the nave
of this now-boarded-up house of God,

where yellow tape surrounds a liturgy
of monochrome—the pulpit embers, the ashen
confessionals, the unburned stone. I drag

a toe beside my bike to slow it down,
and stare at what remains there unchanged:
stone walls, the poured concrete foundation,

an oak close enough to the road to escape
the flames, the sign with yesterday's theme ("He
Is Here") in plastic letters. The wooden beams

have mostly burned away, or fallen inside,
but three angled remnants suggest a steeple,
its point lost somewhere in the drizzling gray.

III.

A quarry of books. In my basement-floor carrel
under shelves of catalogs, I lift
a Chartres photograph up with my thumb

and index finger, careful not to crease
the corner. The cathedral's familiar, old
asymmetries make me tilt my head

sideways. And, here among uneven stacks
of sprawling atlases and journals slim
enough to disappear, I page through

the older fires, short-lived masons, ragged
peasants hauling stones uphill. One spire,
a medieval pyramid, broad-based, and stout;

the other—taller, Gothic, delicate,
and so acute its height appears almost
infinite. I turn the page. A picture

in black and white shot from inside the nave—
the candles, blurred (no flash), and the stained glass,
chiaroscuro, with no narrative—

stops me, and Mary, once in translucent gold,
slips into a gray crowd of angels. The night,
no less than cameras, makes apocryphal

the stories lit by dawn. How many times
did it burn down? And, burned, looking like this
future photograph, who decided what

would stay, what go, this rubble worth rebuilding,
and that detritus swept away? I go
to the top floor to see if I can find

the church on Keswick. How do anomalies
become fixed symbols of the symbols we
inherit, half-destroy, and half-remake?

IV.

A postcard of the Wailing Wall. The atoned push
their scrawled prayers against a wall thinner
than incense. The inner sanctuary (that held

the Covenant inside its box), once hidden
behind a veil, has lost its gilded Ark,
its goat blood, its bells and ropes and candles.

It seems almost deliberate to me—
the crowds thronging this new totem, the outside
of something gone. The wall becomes another

impediment to what does not exist . . .
I tape the postcard by my window. The Keswick Church
across the street has been in ruins for months.

How long before it, too, turns palimpsest?
And when I ask the neighbors, who'll recall
the previous church, the glow? Tucked in a flame:

smaller flames within the fire's wall.

Toward Iceland

for my father

In the blaze of Nordic winter light
on a street with squat crooked houses

you looked ahead at the volcanic blue,
while geese flew over pastel roofs,

and said, I hope when you grow up—
you find a place you love as much

as I do all of this. I was five.
Some nights we'd argue, other days

you'd lift me over sulfur pools,
pretend to drop me in. I'd laugh.

When I was bad you'd put me to bed,
close my door goodnight. I'd promise myself

to stay mad. But the cheerful hum,
the rattle of clumsy breakfast dishes,

the childlike knock, the apple cut
in uneven quarters for me to eat

made me forget, and follow you
with the dim shame of having lost.

Back then, we'd drive past fjords and find
a hidden waterfall by its roar—

we'd stumble forward with misted faces
toward the rocky opening.

Twenty years since your advice
and it eludes me still: I've looked.

Today, you're planting rosebushes,
a star magnolia in the sharp grass

of the garden my mother shares.
Iceland's far away. You cast

a long abstracted look at the blooming
hibiscus, the crabapple tree.

In a blur of mist, the waterfall,
behind its own diffusion, is

only a silver narrow line.

Jacket

She cuts a slim
           physique, cold

in her silk jacket,
           silent and staring.

She's foreign to me,
           photographed,

and wearing a half-lost,
           wily look

I'm told I too
           put on from time

to time. My mother
           has duly mastered

self-willed words
           without a fuss.

Unshelved, she's
           a vision on

a book I browse
           and almost buy.

Haiku for Insomnia

When I couldn't sleep,
the large coffee table book's
unwieldy, chalky,

gorgeous *Edo* prints:
cats gnawing cherry blossoms;
red banners trailing

the confettied streets;
snow lining bark like shadows.
Only time for one,

and I would promise
not to turn ahead. But just
as you were closing

Hiroshige shut,
you would cheat. A rakish grin.
Tomorrow night's will

amaze you. I'm grateful
now you taught me that suspense:
art that waits for you.

Hakafot

—The bride circles the groom seven times in a traditional Jewish wedding

for Sasha and Sam

The white silk tapers down,
like a wishbone, to a point
on her back. He gazes above the crown
of her hair, trying not to watch
her watch him as she drapes the ground
in circles. We watch her touch
the air, and witness a private want.

She looks through eyelet lace,
making sure it's him. Their future
mornings dilate the pillared space.
And could her clockwise steps restore
something of the world? Our eyes
are meant to witness love erase
its holy audience of spies.

Fortune

Sky-blue silk, finicky
as she sewed birds
into the lace, encircling
her fingers like a lover's hair—
beware. Now folded

in small squares in a drawer,
like a letter you reopen
only when possessed
with a need to remember
a particular phrase

that caused you pain.
The sheets for her bed
in a waterproof box
folded and refolded in
ceremonial disuse.

She died of the flu
a century ago. Her sister
married in her place.
Look how much care
and time, you said.

I don't remember the birds,
whether there were flowers,
and if flowers, leaves,
but I see my mother refolding
her great-aunt's sheets,

mummifying the air.
Should we cut a piece,
she asked, and frame it?
It seems like a waste,
those careful stitches

intending the future,
expansive and blessed,
open like a parachute,
as Angelina and her groom
alight, 1919 or so, dizzy

with shared privacy,
desperate not to rest,
but tired as children,
falling asleep,
three-quarters undressed.

III. Trespass

Delay

On this stretch of platform, there is no map.
Just sunlight on the staircase leading up
out of the subway; the mirage of our train
flickering on gray walls, becoming, slowly,
the wrong train, the opposite direction.
Looking down at blackened rails, I wonder,
if someone's bag is ticking, what my last thought
will be. Why has no one tried to kill us?

These past three days I've missed you comically—
I've had to remember to turn when a street ends.
And sometimes when your loss seemed possible,
it blurred the bright green edges of Central Park,
as I walked across from the East Side to the East Side,
head tilted upward, debating things to say.

I've never wanted to die, though I dream, often,
of a shelter from myself. And suddenly
I'm shaking, not from thinking of you, or a bomb,
or any articulate fear, or the oncoming train.
I'm shaking so that I won't disappear.

Pagoda Cinema

Brought over from the former Orient,
this pagoda's become a movie theater now:
a grainy Western preview dubbed in French;
a blue-lit "Latin" love story (expanses
of pixilated flesh tattooed with sub-
titles, the unclaimed skin and sighs quite "real" . . .

except a fly keeps knocking at the screen,
adding beauty marks to ingénues,
or dots of poison to the famous glass
of milk in *Suspicion,* or to arrows shot
by Robin Hood across a studio;
and, drifting into someone's platinum curls,
and dizzy from the film-distorted faces,
or from the speed of now-dead Fred Astaire,
the insect loses us and we forget
again what is and isn't here).

Squatters

We follow signs to an abandoned street
of government-owned homes. Warnings flutter
on trees and boarded-up facades. Doors
blow open on their rusted hinges, screens
as loose as spider webs. The fading paint
flakes off, the walls are gouged, and gold weeds grow
between the floorboards of front porches sunken
from years of alternating sun and snow.

We make sure no one's watching and go in
a house with crooked shelves and a black sink.
We half expect the whole thing to dissolve,
but the roof is sturdy wood. The hearth is lined
with polished river rocks. Abandoned for years,
no trace of squatters. We joke that ghosts,
disturbed out of the dust, could catch us here.
And among the empty rooms, the lamps light up,
the fire snaps awake, and flames appear.

Back at the campground people are still out:
some watch the river from their canvas chairs,
some shuffle cards at folding tables spread
with checkered plastic. When it starts to storm,
we crawl inside our tent, zip up, and stare
at daddy-longlegs shadows on the tarp
as the rain drums. We huddle close to sleep.
Who will go back? Would it be too late?
It's not our job to mop the flooding house,
but we feel the water, and its weight.

Ocmulgee Burial Mounds

for Ryan Wilson

Past shards of bowls, arrowheads, the beads
of a small-wristed gatherer whose teeth
are sown beneath a grass-sealed burial mound,
you lead us. Past a set of panther jaws,
once someone's hat, the deer-bone fishing hooks
pinned behind museum glass, clay dolls
and painted fire: a temple underground,
designed so twice a year the equinox

would light up the chieftain's wood-carved throne.
But not today. Our sun is vulgar, shines
down on the parking lot and flowered mound
alike. We climb. Up here, we're all alone.
It's almost time to go. Remember this scene:
we stand above what's buried underground.

Encounter in East Coker

Humility is endless.
        —*T.S. Eliot, "East Coker," from* The Four Quartets

Outside, the roses fill with rain, and I am close
to weeping in my beer, or—even more grandiose—

telling the Arabic-trained former Iraq soldier,
who lost a piece of his skull, and looks much older

than twenty-two, that love (at least for me) is over.
The night before I played pretend I was his lover,

let him unbutton his shirt and lean against my arm,
as I lay there in my dress. And maybe I kept him warm,

or maybe he cursed the dark hotel room, his body thwarted
by the girl who smoked his cigarettes, the girl he courted

in her bare feet (I kissed him in a side street), who led
him on, now wanting nothing. It's something in my head,

I try to say, as we leave the pub, walking to the church,
the allure of shame or attention; the misguided search

for rapture at all costs. Or is it arrogance?
I loved someone. Now I leave things up to chance.

We find the small church door, right off the cemetery.
I hold his camera for a minute. It's hard to carry.

Hotel Room in Phoenix

Flat champagne on the dresser, bottle rings,
one bra strap looped through the chair back, the other
corkscrewing to the floor—but you're still here,
your cheek against the pillow, mussed hair hiding
an open eye. You show me where to touch you,
what to kiss in the part-dark, acrylic-
curtained room. The morning sun makes squares
on a skyscraper's steel. It's dawn; I think
they're on to us. Your hands smell like dollars;
your eyes are dice.
                        Our crime is far away
from here, and, in the haze just past the canyons,
a moon, clipped, like a silver hair (I find
one in my brush), is a kind of déjà vu.

The Leopard

after Borges

At dawn, the leopard watches the firmament
dissolve in sunlight through his cage's bars;
he's fresh from dreams of tearing flesh, the scent
of deer still on his paws. A carnivore's
nightmare: instead of reddened fields, a cell's
dull iron; of opened rib cages, walls.

If even Dante's waltz can't sidestep fate,
or trick the jailor, then art itself reveals
no door. The leopard roars at the stanza's gate,

claws the corners, scrapes the floor, and steels
himself for solitude. We read our curse
between the lines, vaguely recalling meals

devoured in the wild. No words will quite coerce
these bars to bend, or move the universe.

Trip to Alcatraz

Gulls gathered on concrete in a row
are watching San Francisco's pastels darken
and diffuse in shark-troubled water. When we
draw close (rushed off the ferry with brochures,
sandwiches, and cameras) they stiffen, and show

their silver backs to us. The prison tours
run once an hour, so we leave the birds,
now taxidermy-still, for sound effects
on headphones (squealing steel gates, the noise
of inmates scratching words in these same doors,

the cafeteria brawls over scraps and boys).
Twilight cools the bay and the wind moves
through Alcatraz's iron latticework,
bringing back cold nights when felons played
poker with chapped hands. Remembering joys—

a solo walk, a credit card—we're afraid.
Long, giddy minutes in a bedless cell.
The ferry blares. It's time. Almost last call:
itineraries flutter and the crowd
presses. Digging in pockets for mislaid

ticket stubs. We shuffle on board, heads bowed,
with souvenirs and thoughts of dinnertime.
Fog wreathes the Golden Gate as our boat noses
slowly toward the band of coast. Seagulls
are looping overhead. The waves are loud.

Apocrypha

a medication change—
       lifting the cold soak
of slept-in clothes, raveled
       in the frozen kick of a dream—

and then I have to ask,
       always, did you and I
live together in that house
       with the broken sinks, the windows

looking out at a courtyard
       I remember, but know
I haven't seen, so why
       do I remember? is

it invention? invention
       is maybe something forgotten,
so I invent it again,
       remembering instead

the corners of a room
       I was convinced were also
in your head? and do we conjure
       the past from blueprints we

erased? and who is drawing,
       who is blotting out?
I walk ahead, holding
       a simulacrum of the past

from places I haven't seen
          for people who weren't there
and who when I recall
          our history look blank

bad dream, I will remember you, memorize you, confuse
  you with my life until
someone says, *what do you mean?*   *that never*
  happened   I was never there

The Cut

for S.

Though the pool, already sold, along with the sunlight
lapping over its edges, does not belong to us,
these facts are only technicalities
today: for now, it's ours, in its cool dazzled state
of half-belonging. Wading in just far
enough to be stopped, and gently; held
and holding; pressed against the wall, I'm lifted.

But the rough stone catches on my skin, etches
a shy pain on my spine as you lift me: my body shakes
from the trembling water—from you—again and again.

Below me, with parted lips on my collarbone,
you're not aware of the cut, or the calculus
I made that having you was worth a loss
of flesh so infinitesimal, or how,
for days after I'd touch the mark with the lust
unique to memory, or how I felt
the shrinking cut as a different, newer loss:

if healing is a gradual disappearance,
then I don't want to heal from you.

New Year's Eve

I try to find that quiet bar—the one
    you used to take me to, on a cobbled corner

      by the wharf, shadowed under Federal Hill.
        But I can't find it, or where you always parked.

        I still look for your car wherever I go,
          for a sliver of you in profile, peripheral

to me. I thought I knew this street, but where
    is the water, the tobacco-yellow harbor light,

      the tilted masts, or the old dock wobbling
        under us? I have to remember it all,

        in case: the airport kisses, you, coatless
          in winter, the scent of cold on your shirt, the scent,

somewhere on you, of books. I have to stop
    wondering what you remember. *Here.* Here is

      a different bar: flamingo party hats
        and dollars curled under sucked lemons,

        or stuck to the foam of glasses. Someone kicks
          the jukebox. A hollow laugh, a liquid joke,

and me, wading through last night's balloons.
    This is what it's like now—I hear myself

        explain to a conjured you, the you inside me
            I sometimes talk to—I watch (not always sadly)

            and can't do more. I carry you to places
                where you are theatrically absent. A girl

(she's drunk and pretty) knocks my shoulder, *Sorry,*
    leaving glitter on someone's lips, someone new.

Emily Leithauser was born in Washington, DC, and grew up in Western Massachusetts. She earned her MFA in poetry at Boston University and her PhD in English at Emory University, where she is a Lecturer in the Creative Writing Program. Her work has appeared in *New Ohio Review, Blackbird, Literary Imagination,* and *Southwest Review,* among other journals. She is the recipient of the 2015 Tennessee Williams/ New Orleans prize for poetry. She lives in Atlanta with her fiancé, Simon, and their two dogs.

    The Borrowed World is the winner of the 2015 Able Muse Book Award.

ALSO FROM ABLE MUSE PRESS

William Baer, *Times Square and Other Stories*

Melissa Balmain, *Walking in on People – Poems*

Ben Berman, *Strange Borderlands – Poems*

Ben Berman, *Figuring in the Figure – Poems*

Michael Cantor, *Life in the Second Circle – Poems*

Catherine Chandler, *Lines of Flight – Poems*

William Conelly, *Uncontested Grounds – Poems*

Maryann Corbett,
Credo for the Checkout Line in Winter – Poems

John Philip Drury, *Sea Level Rising – Poems*

D.R. Goodman, *Greed: A Confession – Poems*

Margaret Ann Griffiths,
Grasshopper – The Poetry of M A Griffiths

Katie Hartsock, *Bed of Impatiens – Poems*

Elise Hempel, *Second Rain – Poems*

Jan D. Hodge, *Taking Shape – carmina figurata*

Ellen Kaufman, *House Music – Poems*

Carol Light, *Heaven from Steam – Poems*

April Lindner, *This Bed Our Bodies Shaped – Poems*

Martin McGovern, *Bad Fame – Poems*

Jeredith Merrin, *Cup – Poems*

Richard Newman,
All the Wasted Beauty of the World – Poems

Alfred Nicol, *Animal Psalms – Poems*

Frank Osen, *Virtue, Big as Sin – Poems*

Alexander Pepple (Editor), *Able Muse Anthology*

Alexander Pepple (Editor),
Able Muse – a review of poetry, prose & art
(semiannual issues, Winter 2010 onward)

James Pollock, *Sailing to Babylon – Poems*

Aaron Poochigian, *The Cosmic Purr – Poems*

John Ridland,
Sir Gawain and the Green Knight – Translation

Stephen Scaer, *Pumpkin Chucking – Poems*

Hollis Seamon, *Corporeality – Stories*

Carrie Shipers, *Embarking on Catastrophe – Poems*

Matthew Buckley Smith,
Dirge for an Imaginary World – Poems

Barbara Ellen Sorensen,
Compositions of the Dead Playing Flutes – Poems

Wendy Videlock, *Slingshots and Love Plums – Poems*

Wendy Videlock, *The Dark Gnu and Other Poems*

Wendy Videlock, *Nevertheless – Poems*

Richard Wakefield, *A Vertical Mile – Poems*

Gail White, *Asperity Street – Poems*

Chelsea Woodard, *Vellum – Poems*

www.ablemusepress.com

CPSIA information can be obtained
at www.ICGtesting.com
Printed in the USA
LVOW07s2324140817
545032LV00001B/179/P